COMMUNICATINGROUPS

STU WATSON

Mastodon Publishing
Thoughts Made Real

All Rights Reserved

Printed in the United States of America

First Edition
1 2 3 4 5 6 7 8 9

Selections of up to one page may be reproduced without permission. To reproduce more than one page of any one portion of this book, write to publishers John Gosslee and Andrew Sullivan.

Cover art by Stu Watson
Illustrations by Stu Watson
Interior design by Anna Johansen

Copyright ©2020 Stu Watson

Library of Congress Cataloging-in-Publication Data

2020930569

ISBN 978-1-7334920-0-3

Mastodon Publishing
Thoughts Made Real
mastodonpublishing.com

For special discounted bulk purchases, please contact:
Mastodon Publishing sales@mastodonpublishing.com

To book events, readings, and author signings, please contact:
info@mastodonpublishing.com

COMMUNICATING GROUPS

Ω

fearing commitment and duty
the prince seduced other men's wives
self-delusion always one
of Edward's most powerful allies
insiders: horrified—
the mouth on this flatulent chatter-box
the queen most naturally opposed
their taking any job at all—
I know it's unthinkable, but
we'd probably be looking at
the dismantling of Cutty Sark
centuries, even, before
the arrival of John Cabot—
arctic archaeology
starts with a traverse
sometimes they're described as tiny people
sometimes they're described as giants
they still continue on
in the oral history of the Inuit people
a signature of European occupation
radiocarbon dating measures
the decay of carbon in artefacts
to determine their age
the problem is marine animal fat

the old remains of rendered
animal fat have coated
everything
there will be something earlier
it's primitive but it looks like
it's been worked
the possibility of this area
having been utilized for a period
over four centuries
you would find hones just like that
it becomes
a geography unto itself
under the microscope
tiny traces of metal can still survive
the way that crack cocaine hit
American cities in the 1980s
his actions had an irresistible pull
they reported on his crimes
in minute detail
for ten weeks

there's a lot of concern about lighting
even Queen Victoria approaches
they're cliches, but there's something
almost comforting in this vision
of the East End
vermin, disease, and human waste,
the rain being "scum-filled"
there are rats, there are flies
a dirty secret
and a source of terror
threatening to spill over
steam-powered sewer
pushing everything east
she became a prostitute in Whitechapel
the use of alleyways
a consequence of
the brothels having
been shut down
by new, more moral, laws
it's difficult for them
to get much from
the scene itself
technology about to be born
might have made a difference

the city's police weren't ready
forensic science wasn't ready
it's the night of the 30th
late around one in the morning
number 40 Berner Street
the pony whinnied
wouldn't go any further
no mutilation to the body
an orphan by the time she was fourteen

all that anger was vented on Eddowes
lying on the pavement just there
too many and too disturbing to list
the level of them is intense
the person who committed these murders
didn't have the technical ability
of a horse slaughterer
the truth is far more simple
he wasn't an evil genius
just incredibly lucky
a killer who knew
his territory well
that's all
that the police were satisfied
the murder spree
was over soon after Kelly
was discovered
is either because the killer
died, left the city,
or was imprisoned on
another charge
the reasons for their satisfaction
remain
the cause of speculation

after that one burst
of press interest
the whole thing died—
the city, fortified like
no other, had seemed
impregnable
I was the only one
with courage enough
to bring letters through
the terrible Turkish camp—
just inside the right upright huge
that will make you a few friends
in Philadelphia on top again
back and forth they go
where it stops nobody knows
before it's all said and done
back in the game
he was anxious to get his hands
on another one
a guy named Lucky
would wear 13
whose given name is Rodney
little bit of a weapon for him

Earlier we talked to a man named Julian Pearce, the most in depth account we have heard from an eyewitness. The show was about to end. They shot at us multiple times. It was a bloodbath. I escaped because they reloaded, basically. I just waited for the time they reloaded to climb the scene and to hide behind it. They shot at us for ten or fifteen minutes, it was long, it was very long. About one thousand people can gather in it. It was sold out, basically. It was easy for them. One of the people he was eighteen years old, nineteen years old maximum, twenty maximum, and he was exec-uting people. I have some friends who escaped who heard them talking about Iraq and Syria. I haven't heard anything but the screaming of the people. When you walked in were you searched by security? Nothing, we haven't been searched, nothing. Security was very poor. In the course of ten or fifteen minutes these people were just going around shooting people? Yeah, that's what happened. I was in the front, so I was protected by the bullet. I said to the people around me to calm down and to hide.

Rap against the glass to alert the cashier of your presence and you have run a long career. I was born with the devil in me, and he didn't come rapping inside the smoldering remains of a person tied up in a mattress John Wayne Gacy was responsible for strangling. Gonna take a sentimental journey, put my heart at ease, America's gilded age was booming and the right to celebrate it all. Splendid decadence of Englewood, swollen number of visitors, and Wallace where the money flowed into the old hotel; a tremendous resource, a fascinating mixture of materials, they allow us to travel one hundred years back into the mind of a killer. A killer by whatever means for whatever reasons his style of killing would reflect that obsession with gadgetry. I'm gonna live live live until I die. Three lectures a week on a particular portion of the body. He called all this work ghastly, and lamented the easy path of the rich. The bell began every day, the keeper of the dissection corpses was also, naturally, a trader in wanted and unwanted bodies, even those obtained in a less than legal manner. He was around when bodies came.

Fantasy to a serial killer is the whole foundation of why they become a serial killer. He was able to see the body as a commodity, devoid of anything but mineral value. Imagine, if you will, a table, just like this, a body in between the men twenty to forty hours a week, every week, over a year. Their dream was to take out insurance on a schemer and cash in using a corpse. Much would come of this but not until later, after several bigamies.

I was at last forced to sell my horses, so I began to hunt for corpses, as this scheme called for an extraordinary amount of material, three bodies in fact.

Mudgett then decided to pull off the fraud by pretending to kill only himself. His claim that staring at bodies day after day turned him into a murderer is very curious, because it's obviously at least in part true, though finally it seems his killing was primarily a matter of his direct agency, of his desire for capital. He was possessed of a capacity for unfeeling objectivity, for estimation. His most remarkable trait was his willingness to kill his accomplices seemingly without any trace of moral feeling. The graphic details that he gives of his first victim's corpse are delivered with a knowing melodrama that illustrates his performance of guilt was as much a matter of currency as the killings themselves. He had his own personal form of reality.

Take the bones, articulate them, and you can sell something you were going to throw out. *We have dozens of articulated skeletons around the medical school to this very day.* He ran an integrated operation that culminated in sex murders. He was apparently very handsome and had a great personality. He loved animals so much. He loved to staff his businesses with women, allegedly because he was a great supporter of women's rights. It's unusual, in the annals of serial killers, for the sexual aspect to arrive so late in the process, so to speak. With Mudgett it seems to have grown out of a recognition of his own power over others, as opposed to the power deriving somehow from his desire. Of his desire, beyond the accumulation of personal wealth, we know nothing.

It won't mean anything to him.

He'll kill that child.

He offered her a job in the Castle, and for the next six months he wooed her. When he lost interest in her, he would kill her. If anyone asked, she had left to marry, though she had no wedding, as he gassed her to death when she wouldn't marry him. The wax cylinder confession hints at his motive: he was a compulsive stalker. *We will be happy, Nellie, before we die.* It's unclear how many people he actually murdered. *They asked me the contents of two small barrels and I gave them misleading answers.* He fled with Pitezel, insuring him along the way to Philadelphia, having burned the Castle down before leaving Chicago. He arranged to meet Pitezel again in their newly set up patent office, but instead of using a substitute body as planned, he simply killed him. *I burned him alive. The least I can do is spare my reader a recital of the victim's cries for mercy, which had, on me, no effect.* This is new information.

The
boy's
body he
stuffed
up a
chimney
in
Indiana.

He put
the two
girls in
his
trunk
and
gassed
them.

When
they
were
put
into
the
trunk
they
were
naked.

He shaped an instrument for murder: that was the building. There is something, almost, of bathos in his self-regard; it does not ring true in containing a psyche, his interiority literally pure tabloid, as if he could hear within his own head no other voice than one seeking an audience it despised but had to please and simultaneously defraud and kill.

The only thing
that changes is the
noticing,
our instincts
tell us, this
sort of thing—
killing for
profit of one
kind or
another—has
been going on
since people
first got
together in
c o m m u n i c a t i n
groupsmergedtrib
ewithtribeformed
c i t i e s o u t o f f a m i
liesallagitatedan
imalsleftoutinth
ebargainbutafew
j u s t a f e w g e n e
segotthroughthe
citygatesandnow
wearelefttosortitall
outforourselvesas
bestwecan

It is notable to some, the proximity of the crimes in London to those in Chicago, a few even suggesting the perpetrators were one and the same, various conspiracies to move Mudgett to London from a Philadelphia mental hospital having been floated in an attempt to commodify the notoriety of these events further, to compress the transatlantic emergence of serial murder into a single human source, as if that one set of molecules could "account" for a flaw that was obviously endemic to the genetic code, a flaw so deeply built into what it is to be a person that it may not only be necessary but essential. Some link it to a capacity for abstraction of a particularly distant variety.

The death of Julius Caesar is one of the events of all time. There are many questions left unanswered. Why did Caesar ignore all warnings? *Caesar's assassination is a special case, it presents a challenge, but I'm sure we can use forensic science to determine why, and how, he was killed.* This is also, at its heart, an act of comparative literary criticism, the weighing of all the relevant ancient sources. Using computer generated models we will recreate the crime scene, which today is covered over by a curved alleyway and a rounded building whose walls bend where the Theater of Pompey once stood. How could such a man, who was always prepared, be so unprepared? Or was it a kind of suicide by senator? What did Caesar really think about himself? Did the conspirators actually mastermind his murder, or were they then, as before, merely Caesar's pawns in an elaborate game whose design still remains veiled by the distorting lenses of historians and artists? It will be unclear.

He rises from an old family that has seen better days. Though he writes prolifically about himself and his accomplishments, he never mentions his epilepsy, what Shakespeare calls his "falling sickness." That his writings exist entirely as propaganda, both for his contemporaries and for us, is clear. The senate was meeting at Pompey's Theater because their traditional home had burned and was in the process of being reconstructed. Was this burning the first stage of the conspiracy? How long was the con? We record the crime scene to aid in our analysis, to add to the computer generated model. How many of them were directly involved in the assassination? How could they keep such a secret with so many conspirators, so many wavering loyalties?

His home has only recently been identified; it now stands, a complex ruin. The autopsy reports he was stabbed 23 times, though only one of the wounds was deemed by the doctor to have been fatal. Does this imply that there were 23 conspirators, or is it possible there were many more who in the mad rush failed to get in a cut? A crowd of 23 people is radically impractical for this kind of thing, even 11 men, if human nature holds across the generations, are far too many for this number of wounds. It seems likely there were possibly as few as 5 conspirators who actually did the stabbing, while the others watched out for witnesses, ran crowd control, interference with Caesar's bodyguards. All the reports indicate it was an incredibly chaotic scene, a frenzy more animal and brutal than anything seen on the contemporary stage.

Gaius Cassius Longinus was alleged to be a "hot-tempered gambler." He fought against Caesar in the civil wars, but, perhaps recognizing his ambitions, Caesar forgave him this and promoted his position in the senate. A notorious womanizer, Caesar had previously slept with Brutus' mother, Brutus dogged by rumors of bastardy, though the dates don't work—— these two began to recruit | other disgruntled youthful | senators, those snubbed | that day some weeks before | when they made Caesar | a living god | he didn't stand | perhaps embracing his new godhead | performing the gift he'd just received | though of course | Cassius Dio claims Caesar was suffering | from terrible diarrhea | or as Plutarch has it | an epileptic fit | which culminated in | him screaming | "Kill me now! I won't resist! | Kill me now! I won't resist!" | while baring his throat | to all the senators who assembled | which account we can believe | we must decide for ourselves.

Caesar's temporal lobe epilepsy was gradually getting worse. It seems likely the epilepsy induced in him a state of constant agitation, a low-grade mania that can be used to retroactively account for his prolific activity as a writer, sexual being, and conquerer. Brutus stabbed him in the groin. The conspirators took to the streets, proclaiming their victory over tyranny. Caesar must have known about the conspiracy to kill him. He deliberately provoked his enemies by means of public insults. Was his death the suicide of a sick and dying man? Or was there more to it? Was this suicide, thus, entirely rational, despite its being exacerbated by the irrational inducements of his illness? Was his death motivated by a desire for the eternal fame he surely achieved? What is fame to a dead man? Within three years of the murder, all the conspirators were dead. His selected heir, Octavian, was judiciously chosen, to say the least. In this way, even through his own death, Caesar can be said to have won, and had Antony defeated Octavian at Actium, the same could still be said, for Antony was also Caesar's blood. His genes survived, maintaining a stranglehold on power in Rome for a century until at last, it seems, the madness finally won out, though we cannot say that is what really happened with any certainty.

Martha Tabram,
stabbed more times than
Caesar, not remembered
but for other murders
in her neighborhood, her death
a happenstance
ocurrence
documented retroactively
in case it might prove to be
a clue in the best-selling
historical mystery—bayon-
ette through, brute way
to die.

Can scientists learn from the unflinching accounts of men like him? The raging thirst, the fever, the delirium, and most of all, the agonizing black swellings.
In its final stages, the bacteria mutates into *pneumonic plague*, which has a mortality rate of almost ninety percent, at least theoretically. In actuality many unexplainable immunities obtained, mutations perhaps from earlier undocumented plagues we don't remember except inside our bodies | outside language.

Edward VIII had no children
with Mrs. Simpson, so
his brother's daughter
would have reigned
no matter what—Mudgetts
still survive, perhaps Jack's
family as well, we cannot
say who lives through a plague, the
genes of murderers outlasting
those of celibate saints,
the link between immunity
and morality a haphazard logic
running streams of shampoo
squeezed and eddying in a drain

———in the blank afterwards

layers of moralizing enfolding and crushing horror to use it
the agenda best that squeezes water most
the rinds drowned in desiccation all these viruses | virtues
flush indoors now and sweep the bad shit out
use our bodies most
we with immunities
we haven't earned
our genes one way
not another out of
mere chance and not
some scrupulous
knowing empathy
nothing moral in any most
clawhammer-disclose the street beneath sheetrock
underground river of pavement the knock-kneed shake at
bramble of a wire tangle torn up by a digging steam-engine
powered by petrol pumped out of whale gut strung violins
and lyres wires tensing further as the toothed bucket digs in
the pulling out by the root of our connections stems no
dream tides corrupt as a singular blemish on a model's mouth
you dread the fortitude it will take to endure so many more
years of incessant screaming born of actual pain and
righteousness

3

The Will to Know

It's a barbarian's dream just to speak the language, and we know this, shocking him at every turn, behind his back as once we could be said to have baked walnuts accidentally amidst the horrors of the bread factory fire, toast smell in that whole village for a week until the squall came in at last and ripened up the air enough to rinse it out. That cleansing has now been marked a part in a limited series, salmon skin seared perfectly until there's no more salmon in the sea, that sort of edge off of which our ship is sailing, a waterfall of darkness leading down to an expanse that promises no space for anyone. Clouds on the fat-turned Earth still spool in marble oceans up but what's the process worth if at one end it drools itself out over all our laps in smog? Completer pictures of a barren desert required. The rhetoric was finally drained when it was taken out of education, as though we almost knew that that would happen, though it happened anyway as a part of a global process running since before the first man spoke, where is the agency, the nature of the tie between biology and will, that is, what forces do we shape as much as find their ends in us? That in the light of a closely glorious doom, in bloodshed under progress, how many more of us will stand up with the laser ready to lance corporeally down, to boil out our indolence and act without close comfort in our rectangular electrical torches? What is ultimately more impotent than a moral bully? Of consequence or not, who stakes dispersals when the boxes fill? Grape leaves burst along the vein lines when overstuffed I learned the hard way when first an intern in the kitchen, compulsorily an intern in an effort to teach me more than I would learn, in an attempt to indoctrinate me with a desire to serve I already seemed to possess as a primary guilt formed on the first opening of eyes, the apology for witnessing the light itself, good lot. A form of guilt beyond bad faith whose other side is a brooding and compressed authority of its own, the process of slipping under at the edges of our era, this process we are undergoing inside ourselves, reconciling individual nature with how alike we all are, our wishes and our bodies under blade or bomb blast at the reckoning ground where ideology becomes mechanical violence or deliverance. A hyphenated knowing aimed at both sides, curious to say, the idea that perception might merge totally with analysis, that seeing might be reading, actions might be words, the league of all connection just the shimmering magnitudes of electrical pulses delimited by the lengths of fiber-optic thread, by how many electrons we can successfully hypothesize at once as reference points for memories, sub-atomic oscillation in and out of ratiocination and in clearing up and on into a vivid ocean floor, a ground unmolested wholly by the actions of desire.

The Amerika Rocket

Upon being ordered to the Alps, the preparations continued as before, making missiles in the mines, and the missile making hasn't stopped and we have reached the poem, the edge of our basic gravity, reflections in the lunar months unfastened and men and women live now up beyond the reach of tides. Eisenhower's main thrust was to the south because he feared a prolonged guerrilla action in Bavaria apparently more than he feared the Soviet occupation of all of old Prussia, perhaps internally understanding the way a corrupt dictatorship must ultimately crumble, himself wrapped up no doubt in empirical considerations we can no longer even imagine correctly by reading the numbers, lacking any real feeling of pressing consequences, lacking a sense of the game, of these numbers as part of a system still in action, though of course they are, each single casualty reshaping in its way a bit of history, each death a blank end to generation born thousands of millennia before, when rats were young, that without his decisions otherwise might have thrived continuously through this very moment. Of course subscribing unto Eisenhower agencies like these comes with its cost to us as well, we individuals most often blithely unaware of where we stand, of how much meaning our actions and our words really project out there, in space. The goal of his drive south, of course, was space, space in the form of men who could make rockets strong enough to propel us out of gravity, although as fate would have it the Soviets achieved this with Sputnik before the Americans under Eisenhower could manage, even with the brain of Wernher Von Braun on their side, Von Braun who was captured in Bavaria, working, as he had been, on the V2 which still looms so large in the imaginations of those who lived in London during the war, but also on another, grander project, what seemed then surely a delusion. The final dream, the one of the true fanatics like Goebbels, the one Von Braun was working on so diligently in his mineshaft, was of a rocket that could reach New York or Washington from its Alpine launching zone, possibly underground, or in a mountain hollowed out from above, a kind of natural silo. This hypothesized "Amerika Rocket" is of course what would become the Saturn V, launched not from Bavaria but Florida, so in a way its name turned out to be perfectly appropriate but for reasons totally at odds with the intended ends of the original namers. So it will have been with all naming.

Rodan

When in the tunnel one embodies a third way, a wild space of bodily breakage where the one hand grips the other grips the other overhand and where the agent where the object starts remains innate, inchoate, and at least electrically eliciting some knowledge apprehended without clean shape or fringeless edge where all contact is as abrupt as a rough drip from off an overhanging air conditioner prepared to tumble from its perch, gilled with freon. Our hot spells commence with newest agitation as the trains whirl just to fall back into longing from a door stoop when the brawl exceeds the boundaries of the sidewalk flatly, crowning this achievement with a bliss made violent, slow shudder until the water cannons reenact the buried rivers, miserable as scars touching a lava lamp, this question of contingency of subject yes of object, this partible conjunction of new lies particular in any other case turned general in this correct deduction. More routine than leaving and more comforting than being held with love, the distance from ourselves we are pulling ourselves open just to see, like hanging veils of moss before an aperture of vines with licorice inwoven, confections here the mark of all this, more than rebar or t-bones of new hewn steel, the powdered sugar an epoxy grit more truculent than concrete but breathed clean through as when a gravel pit submerges itself in a sea of tar but still lends character to the new road, a layering of peas beneath the newest tarmac mattress way. And easy as it is to blame a government, in the case of most disease the panic is not rational but like a glare that stands you through matched perfectly to all you do not need, so much alike as to be finally the same, beyond the clone where newer motions meet in a glum fist that raps upon a solid door to reach back just enough to make it sync, the land's volumes attuned to this, to her, to that cinematic who strains at the captured sun's reign, those crueler guides hold hands up and don't shout right, we reminded ourselves both to feel our weight as armor against jagged cuts and slashed so that stabs are all we need to watch out for, unless they open up the gate to all animals at once, and also to bear ourselves carefully as we tread upon tracks flipping in a journey, when you take the shortcut that way, son, you'll never be a leader.

Chandeliers

Collapsed lung pavilion where they keep the hiving hobbies of the weak toned bright enough so as not to drive out fully a mete despair, this vestibule contingent with so many ways contending all at once all at the, ah, brink of some raw moment catching finally in your throat not just with beauty there but in an actual sadness closing off intestinal tube-ways, armies of embarrassment and of endorsement also, gripping in the pit a bell-like voice at its numb source before it screams, a waiter's angry awkwardly you are alone and do not drink but linger silent at the Rome cafe embracing in your thin way energy you need and suck in all the oil of the fine, generic noodle. Semantics of the body across language ring you in tones clear enough to bother with when naked new and neat across the way in an undark room the curtains' muslin dyed a ribboned shade of burgundy and your hands shake as you feel time slip, accessories of drama and the clambering intense and dirty dream pits, whips crack and the carriages in barrage after barrage slope by the dark wings clacking you look out your window see the world spurt by on horseback roll yourself into a ball and flex your legs beneath the threadcount. No hands were sharpened pulling just together these miniscule knots, and you know that I am not the type to say this sort of thing but this time it really matters so you all better do something before it is too late and I've held off until just now to tell you out of taste but now the time for being cool has closed at last and you must place yourself and your belief there at the risk of sounding as if such a thing might ever be believable and not in and of itself another act, a game slipped into and embraced as if the real like all real things are all real things we have led ourselves now to believe, dragooning a militia of our mind's eye into what we can still capture and contain from our own past, lies dazzling enough that we don't miss their arc cascading downward on our eyelids slammed quite closed. In all the things you wanted to be free and now you are so let the symmetry of sometimes ugly reason leave enfolded in an envelope you seize from off the bureau by your long new bed where lying down you feel completed, bred, fool in love with everything again now not complaining now feeling horizons as no limit to your journeying across the well-honed crisis tackling jostling rivers of words all in discordant shape under each side, an augur of evaluation's shade, you crop your hair from photos in blind rage as singing sirens startle you aware of who you once pretended that you really were, complaining that way to that broken staring parking lot attendant with a limp, oblivious to everything but the creed his radio emits, emulsifying a crackle there out of the sky unmarried but intangible. It's then you think that a machine has woven every sheet you've ever known, that nowhere in the world right now are hands whose work has closely, tenderly created what the world needs and you want to vomit at your own egocentricity but also know that this awareness cannot even hold you long enough in its embrace to begin to speak about how one might make a difference if you do not let it in at all and are content to monitor in darkness your nice dreams ensuring you have never exited a stratosphere of openness or laughed too loud like a grunge rockstar buying all of Francis Bacon on a whim or every strategy you promulgate for winning at a pure game of chance in total knowingness but without irony or any secret purpose but a purer need. The light thrown always moving round in circles with the wind illuminates the alley afterimage slowly, unfolding rather like an accordion impossibly compressed or like a collapsible pitchfork ready to sell at an outrageous markup on the corner of a riot, where the riot meets again the stillness of the sidewalk that it occupies, that stillness present even in the mess of noise made visible in the circling halos of beams that find us in our homes ready or not so pretty in our estimation if we let go into really seeing where all beauty lodges which of course we don't do out of courtesy but need for our own sense of having repeated the steps as directed over and over. A certain surname leapt off of the page which was as easily fixed as finding a new apartment in the city could have been if we'd obeyed our instincts and not listened to an arrogated reason, as is always tempting when pressed by time and circumstance, by sale of space and rule of movement and the close geometry of boxes, couches turn into an encumbrance beyond all the being they bear up in sad after glowing sex light on the drastic shifts of certainty around each turn and how the greatest are nonplussed by pain as if it were a part of plans that we're not privy to and won't be until it's long over and unground we're dead to rights caught looking at the thing we most desire and the person feels desire and can only be disgusted in a recognition of the fraught distractedness it stands for when reconsidered on its own outside the course of other real events suspended from the ceiling filled with dust, melted grains of stone that clatter and might crack and break apart if you just drop them. Of course what the dictator wanted above all else was power, and oddly that is not always obvious of a dictator, though in the course of time it is born out, enlightenment being finally a sham, or finally, at least, a place that none can act from in a way that this firm truth they have consumed is likewise universally revealed, for if some cannot feel for it, a missing link emerges, and from these broken ties come swells disrupting clean consumption of the jagged, unpredictable new light. And with a gesture animals will know what you might do, will read into your shoulder turn the possibility of feeding. This is natural but we also know that it is a behavior we ourselves conditioned, unconsciously, in the simple act of providing a life with shelter and with food.

Big Pressures Were There

They would have had a terrible time living virtually anywhere, because they grew out of a piece of history that they were not involved in, a kind of ultimate abjection, so deep that a lawyer shields them from all contact, a goose wing for these ducklings, though no governor dare risk the generosity that could admit them to the space, now incognito, whether they died without issue in 1960 sorrowing or are survived by sons in the United States, the relative's shadow can never leave them, bearing them always into a repository of filth and simplicity beyond all reckoning, a veritable black hole of process mapped against the rate of limiting change and then fed back as in a loop, regurgitation of self-genesis new normal in a life of infinite regress, regression towards a blither dawn that riddles circumventing audiation placid as a person with not a thing to eat or drink and you have all the most expensive liquor in the still blooming broken chore inflexible and always a source of trouble not to be fraternized with at any cost because they do not deserve any sympathy, they just deserve the watchful aloofness of lovers certain of deception but not certain of the other's certainty. You just kept quiet, everybody knew it had happened a lot, but you just kept quiet. We were the losers. Everyone knew what had happened to us, and as a result there was no way in, no way, even recognizing our humanity, to satisfactorily respond when plunging over and over again into a darkness beyond which the law, itself just that which we have all agreed upon tacitly or not, can be seen finally outlined with thinning orange flames as of a bird tail blooming in a fan in a castle on the Turkish coast, the lagoon below already full of European pleasure yachts. The day he died the first communists were flown into Berlin, the exiles who had long been training back behind the lines for just this purpose, the political rebirth of a whole nation and in the process a total reform of a state so thoroughly debauched as to be a byword for debauchery itself beyond all limit, and for all appearances of voting they must hold it hand in hand grip all their hands and squeeze them onto what becomes the process, offering them positions that they could easily manipulate, municipal king-making to begin the reformation or the punishment which of course are endlessly implicated in and by each other if one steps back into the depths of the present forest's perspective, keeping the peace like the distant abstraction we aspire to be, a virtual mass of red tape in triplicate, the sprawling out of permits from a wildly overabundant control commision stocked five times fuller than even America's mixed-up lot of looters running rampant. Over a shattered land the meta-shaking of the idea of power loosened nothing as the fragileness of orbit resides and fuels on fusion newer meadows, Berlin Spring illusions of Stalinist thaw to drink in a deception deeper intention behind a system that is not completely rigged as a new jib planted on a pole inside a shopping cart, silk sail dragging the uneven wheels along the pavement in drunken gulps, guffaws of breeze tipping the cart over and spilling the dazed tank top wearing passenger there hard onto the California pavement in the suburban parking lot next to his uncle's Lexus parked there as he gets his groceries all unaware. The uncle, equally ashamed, imparts to us this wisdom: in looking back on former enemies you now serve, never let an officer complain, or you will find yourself smiling into oblivion. For no one then could tolerate the seriousness we actually felt both reveling in our guilt and suddenly quite conscious that we more than deserved the things that fell on us even if our individual will was of a separate order altogether from those, largely dead but also here among us everywhere, who will not even acknowledge their complicity at all in this process for which we are all paying now, this appalling draining out of dignity, this sieging of the local women, and there's a handsome American so, why not? It would be very nice, but they weren't well-liked, and human nature being what it is, all these people would date, it's automatic isn't it, there were lots of very pretty girls we were not permitted to fraternize with but of course that dissolved itself into a dew and we lived very intensely having filled a massive stadium for our effort. Whether from England or America there was a tremendous amount of food outside the walls, and all came out to acquire what they could afford, but eventually she came to a realization, telling her husband in an intimate moment "You can give me a palace here, I do not care. I'm going back to Germany." In this individual case we find more people in the British Zone than any other, the situation reaching a new crisis having returned in the dark, murderous winter, cold closing in on all of us and the accumulations of ice so great no wood could burn and thousands froze to death besides their empty oven doors, graves dug with dynamite or the superabundance of grenades and ordinance that had been left yet unexploded. Despite all this there was no coal, and all around the industries collapsed at a new rate. A British agent claimed a group of hidden saboteurs were preparing to infect the entire world with a frightening new disease, but this, of course, was mostly an exaggeration meant to justify a continued occupation, the threat of weapons of mass destruction already having become a fast excuse for utterly repressive actions, the threat of mass political assassination the closest expedient at hand, and we are never privy to the details of all the prisoners and for this reason end up blaming ourselves as the innocent hang and the gangs of collusion sail on underneath the scent accurate demarking will allow given that people and allegiances do not always cohere into subjection until the engagement has begun as nothing shows more readily than how these factories of death were here deployed by a few brutal gangsters we all enabled and abetted, worshipped, loved, put all our hopes in, more than anything, and now live with that as we all live with the consequences of our having taken up that one baton that time and struck the band to order blaring order in our wretched homemade uniforms. But really, more than anything, it was the circumstances, more than anything. I guess what I mean is *you had to have been there and you weren't anyway and so there is no chance of us relating to each other the best that we can hope for is we don't force each other to starve.* Athelstan had all the charm and all the verve of an American President, and many different people stood poised to contest for supremacy, the winner's prize an early empire in Britain, a union beyond Wessex, Mercia, and the Danelaw—this new country would then grow to include Wales, Scotland, and Northumbria, with Ireland left waiting for when the work had all been done. A thirty year old king, Athelstan swept Britain in what historians would call, inaccurately, a blitzkrieg, important term from the 20th Century, a term quite inappropriate, considering the Vikings they were fighting and the utter lack of lightning, thunder, any form of fire, or of flashiness of any other kind except the dull glint off sharpened steel blades drawn to hew men down. Then Athelstan subdued the five Welsh kings, made them his newest vassals, finally crushing the last of the Cornish lords, though most men have forgotten that Cornwall was once a country of its own. In this way England was invented, and all are better for it. He left a personal written testament besides a saint's tomb as Alexander might have visited an oracle, the saints the by-far-most-pagan-part of Christian culture in the medieval era, power on earth residing in the orb and cross as it had at least since Constantine, Justinian's statue then still standing in Constantinople, a statue possibly at least twice life size which loomed near the Hippodrome whose one raised portion is still visible today beneath a modern school where every morning children gather to be instructed in the ways they are to value and evaluate the world. Soliciting the aid of the Northern Saints, the expedition traveled further into Scotland than anyone since Agricola nearly one thousand years before, and strange to say, the Scottish kings capitulated and were reinstated, the navy moving onward to ravage the northern coasts and Orkneys. The river was a little trickle, with a sheepbridge left over for some centuries, and there you see the hedgerow, which has grown since Anglo-Saxon times, which row demarks the hard edges of the old estate set up by Athelstan upon his conquest of this region, the land still holds the scars, in form of tree and brush, of hedgerow lines he drew delimiting the power of men he had subdued, could draw out of the earth. The pain of this was huge for our family, a public humiliation that has stood the test of time, glasses, looking like Harry Potter, my last uncle just wanted to do what was right, he was an honest and kind, caring person, and even though his past was truly painful you could feel the real emotion, tragedy all the way around, the way all young dreams nurtured eventually grow into a nightmare of one form or another, especially when they are completely and specifically realized. Athelstan died a bachelor in 939. Pouring rain implies an agency from above that is finally just precipitation, part of the chaos working itself in and out in all air constantly, the hanging of power on one being, however imaginary, always an oversimplification, as Athelstan found out, his brother the cruel Edmund taking over, eventually losing all the gains as temporary structures do not long outlive their architects, the general swell of divergent pressure zones, nimbus cumulonimbus mammatus harbinger of swells of milk, revulsing Athelstan, his name some patronymic trace, not the other Indo-European root meaning "land" we are familiar with from recent eastern wars, that is to say endeavors in liberation from an ideology so easily othered except when we find it in ourselves, in our disgruntled children, children anathema to Athelstan, himself a terrorizer, especially, of the young, though women seem not to have feared him personally, perhaps because his interests naturally inclined in a different direction, though the chronicle is not clear if that was really the issue, or if it was instead some other genetic problem we won't learn of until we have thoroughly tested his bones, having unearthed them from their resting place at Malmesbury, his burial there and not at Westminster a final hint of his essential alienation from Wessex, a realm that had been meant for a brother who died only weeks after receiving his inheritance in circumstances that remain veiled to us, lost on burnt pages of the chronicles, but which circumstances we can assume, left a bad taste in all of Wessex's mouth.

Misspelled Name Love Note

The Plantagenet on the table of the laws | with all his moxie and his flaws | dynamite of generations gone | bearded face that children smile upon | armed bodyguards around you every evening | the loaves and patterns weave and bring | combustion artificially to flame | the stars all terrified as if all stars the same | attract dark murderous obsession | when that is just potential that might lessen | as the fusion fuel starts to slip | the arbitrary speculative bubble of the hour drip | its ooze in gushes | igniting water in plasmic steam that rushes | all burns clean | mums mean | business | less | these days | than they used to, eh? | a man so angry did not | receive a return call when he got | the hospital on the line | they'd spelled his name wrong and by the time | they went to call him he had shot | the hospital all up in a white hot | rage | page | out of Charles Whitman's book | that man who in the 1960s took | to a tower in Texas and inaugurated | this flood of public violence which even now has not abated | though if you look in closer you might see | it really all began with Kennedy | assassinated on display | while waving there in Dallas that fall day | the bitter Oswald in the sixth floor window | prepared to show | us all | his gall | from the school book depository | farcical end to an uplifting story | the way a sudden absence shines too bright | igniting feelings, eradicating night | how all forget the edges where unclear | but real ambiguities work, at play there near | the skin, the surface mediating between will | and fate, between our freedom and the ways we still | submit unwittingly to processes we think we choose | a strong illusion, difficult to lose | becoming dependent on the world we build | that builds us too by means of highly skilled | and profitable super- and sub-structures spread | throughout our sight, words, longings, dead | or living, all must feel its grip | the pressure of the world makes all seams rip | bursts any preconception not arranged | in ordered pre-set patterns that can't be changed | the way misspellings tip your hand | for some, reveal you haven't planned | for serious mess adequately | are not well-schooled in this propriety | while at the other end is emphasized | a freedom from authority that's prized | above all else, a greatest virtue | and what is a confused outcast to do | the kind who in his love note to Madonna cannot | even spell her name correctly though he's not | thought | of aught | else for weeks | compulsively he seeks | her out believes he marries her | from that point on continually harries her | until he finally is shot | while breaking into her California home. She's not | there when this happens but has by then already been | quite traumatized by notes he has sent in | said notes containing many crude mistakes | Madonna spelled Madnna, and the like, this takes | us right into his warped worldly conception | where all convention falls to self-deception | delusion drawing patterns from thin air | perceiving things that simply are not there | could never be | based only loosely on reality | where come these violent bursts | these frothing lips, these thirsts | but somehow from within us where | dirt meets the bottom of the basement stair | the trapped dog digs up seeking how | to circumvent the circumstance of now | though how's a dog to know the house is girded round | some feet beneath the basement ground | with an impenetrable though thin | veneer of nanotubes that will let nothing in.

Unaccounted For Circuit Flip

He also tempted people with cheap gems and stories of adventure. It was a particularly savage crime, the bodies found stabbed, burnt beyond recognition, no longer just a conman and thief, he flees Bangkok and travels to Nepal with his two accomplices. | He saw tens of millions of people denied the basic necessities of life. | Anyone can be a stalker, and anyone can be a victim, it doesn't matter if you're a celebrity, anyone can fall prey to this, anyone, although I've only had three stalkers that frightened me, we had a brief encounter, she was gay and she was attracted to me, she started to become sexually aggressive, possessive, and although we had seen each other only three times in person, I knew it was something I didn't want to be involved in, she didn't want to hear that I wasn't interested, she was already involved, my life having become the object of her life, a cascading set of reflections and imitations, I'm going to torture her mentally she told my friends, there's no possible way it had to be an inside deal the phone company insisted, you really know how to hurt a person she said, over and over this kind of thing would go on throughout the day and night, one time as I was about to board a plane my phone would not stop shaking for the messages and when I shut it off to board the plane and fly across the Atlantic Ocean it was a relief to know there would be silence for some three weeks, and that maybe, when I returned she would have gotten over it, because I was beginning to fear for my safety, but when I returned there was the sound of possums under the floor, the clanging of old pipes, I'd had possums there before but this was somehow different and when the exterminator arrived he said that something had been down there but something quite a bit larger than an opossum or even a pack of them, she then began to break into my bathroom when I showered, the police were reticent to get involved, despising homosexuals then as everyone did, openly, but when she smashed my window with her hand and shoved her face, cutting her cheek, through the cracked and broken glass, screaming incessantly for several hours, they finally arrested her, though she was out within the week of course, and the threats immediately escalated, a new level of violence beyond the glass shattering and screaming, this person hasn't threatened your life, there's nothing that we can do, you haven't been harmed bodily, you're on your own it's getting too intense | seven months of silence | my housesitter discovered her inside my house when I | was off again in Turkey | then seven page letters every week defaming me | to all my friends | my business contacts | seemingly everyone I'd ever cared about at all | describing me as this disgraceful lesbian | having stolen my rolodex and sent these letters | she was finally arrested | immediately made bail | arrived with two guns one pointed directly at her head | she took my three friends hostage | surrendered after eleven hours | you never know who it could be | so impossible to anticipate if it will happen to you | like a random falling object | there is no adequate preparation | save avoiding any attachment at all | which is, of course, its own reward.

Keith Hernandez Popcorn Voyeurism

An all-too-human fascination with evil, with seeing actions as evil, with seeing things we envy as being somehow bad, inversion suddenly the seemingly natural course for things, turns everything back on its own initial orientation, like the desperate urge among European ethnicities in America to claim that it was actually their ancestors who were the first to arrive intent on completely despoiling the land and killing the local peoples, this point of pride in being first overriding completely the content of that priority, and this sort of structure we see reified again and again in revolution after revolution succumbing to the pressures of internal incoherence, to the push and pull of needs that rises in one when a long struggle has finally been seemingly redeemed. The thing that sells is not the fully exposed, unadulterated product, the commodity unmagnified, but rather that which is gradually unveiled with the most nonchalant but totalizing foresight, the plan that comes upon one almost like nature at its most pleasant, a dumb, sustaining beat. There's something comforting in tasks that are just difficult enough, that do not demand one really stretch wittingly beyond what one finds to be a personal limit. Watch as he automatically munches and imagine him doing it over and over again, perfecting his adumbration of future pleasures when he invariably remembers this later, either in onanistic solitude or perhaps while with a partner, the particular limitations inherent in a body's vicinity being after all no limitation to one capable of abstract imagining, of calling up the past, of figuring the future. When this capacity for abstraction comes up against a lack of regard for the differences between the imagined and the real, as in the imposition of a vision for growth by a parent on a child, but also as in many other areas, there the instability of one's worldview borders on Pyrrhonism, that is a skepticism that pushes up against the border between reality and dream, positing that, ultimately, the differences are immaterial, and with this separation goes first a kind of self-regard, a capacity for protectiveness, for seeing one's own value in a sea of sudden non-meaning, what stands in then for value is just pleasure, pure nodal yearning, and this begets addictions of all variety, for the body is but the seat of a mundane animal longing at its base unless an enormous amount of conscious strain is willingly undertaken to break through the will and enter into a level of awareness out-sizing the polygonal sides of three-dimensional vessels. The vilification of voyeurism sees a form of seeing as wrong but in seeing this is implicitly also indicted for the crime it identifies.

Clarence Thomas Coke Can

The meeting place of two distinct crises, the place where two roads meet, the meat of the matter, the cross, where the divergent forces of the structure come together and combine, is always, as they say, the place where tragedy arises, the source of our need for repetition, for all a road implies is repetition, that someone else has gone this way before, that many people have over days or years all beaten down this course into a path in a very needy way in any case for long enough someone has perhaps "improved" the road so that armies of soldiers and goods might cleanly traverse the distances between the built up crossroads we call cities. The family of origin is middle class suburbia and that is a major commonality in all of their M.O.'s, these figureheads we look to when we have become allergic to depth, when we need to cover over a gaping and possibly irreparable gap in the idea that governs us, a gesture that reinforces the fracture it claims to heal, like a peculiar architecture designed only to crash into the ground interestingly, a suite of destruction constructed by unstructured design if without full knowledge of what the mind is conflating as it flies, the idle distraction of a powerful man entranced by the thing he personally desires when just over the ridge of his perspective: a goal beyond possible imagining, a potential buoying up out of the collective sea that bursts a carbonated bubble near the bent-in aluminum tongue, crackling with effervescence in as old containment is eliminated. A trail leading directly to a river, leading directly to an ocean, through the woods and shelves of bamboo, at the edge a final flight of dunes, and then, with military precision, into the briny water open armed as eroded copper lines shine green through the cliffs leaking a greenness across the sand in the dull ceramic glaze of an element making a break for metallic life. Ox eyes looking inward at the plow, the darker earth emerging as the field turf breaks away, the wave pressures particularized in the bodies of the team of beasts, the energy in transit through the play of transformation, this simple act of linkage giving birth to all the nations, to the language and the words we use stretching beyond the limits of our lean native geographies. The exchange of words was born from the exchange not just of goods but of course of people, of women kidnapped forced to adjust to the ways of a suddenly different world, find common groups of sounds that could be understood, used to convey the basic necessities of personhood that even then were evident and palpable as now. These words, in all likelihood, were terrified at first, ejaculations and protestations of fear, words screamed against the violation that was the necessary part of this procedure from the captor's perspective, whatever need was motivating this drive for "cultural expansion." How did this change or is every language marked by these exchanges, bred out of these conquests into this ocean of significance we are flung into, our bodies just beyond the limitations of the tongue somehow the tongue part of the body all the body's flaws in all the breaks and gaps that come from speech. And in all the lore of ancient Canada before it had that name before it had any recorded name we nonetheless hear of migrations in the stories that are passed down, of different groups of people marked out as monstrous and while it remains unclear exactly who these people were, what migration this was, this prophecy of horrible things to come hits history's vital vein. All we have left is memories upon which to base our judgements, along with writing, and we know these memories are not only completely fallible but also subject to the dictates of individual belief, like words, to the strength of each particular person to generalize out of his or her experience into an universal law and this ability is broken across all minds, across all groups of genes, across all individuals who remain members of a class, and this is something that has its element in the empirical universe and yet we act as though a pure concept of law can not only be reached but embodied in a panel of the righteous. Haunting reflections about the unborn and the dying while the living go on monitored: stasis-not-transition, as if states had not their own ridiculous waste, as though memory and language were separate categories of experience as open and porous to infection by the will as any other area of life, we can covet a better past and eventually come to believe we lived it, because we said so, just as a neighbor's wife can come to covet us.

A Thousand Times Before

it's everything you want to say I understand and am agreeable to comply because by now the light has burned me so I cannot propositionally logic backwards through the portholes to points where I might only hypothesize this awkwardness now fuschia felt across frequency ranges from off my cheeks and in this watershed I fear marathons athwart me rushing crowded horde towards skin's plateglass limits barrages the pheromones takes walled up so clutching towards good blockage ladles out ripe mouths schismaticized at a cross of street ways light-held wire drapes sling up sag eyes roll slow slump back in blood rushing catapults of pulp board filigree ideals inside her furniture now sing lifting new bottles out their whirring sand spun decanters marbled through with shades of bend come lysosome tracked car scorn chip pump of new wine cranked angle sends incertitude through rhythms cloying nocte tua morte mio as in that last embrace so flannelled over in the gray lights of Woonsocket by fisher-cat-strewn meadows where a golden houred golf course might have stood moss dripping motivated slung down as with real vigor and underneath it all the years for me the unsettling knowledge of hollow impermanence and doom that things could not even begin to work and now the angle of time clears us of grave attractions slowly ghoulishness of death in pleasure etc it comes across much differently then when it is you as the animals all die and drift away and continents of plans spool into the carriage house made now your home descending into a space of former grandeur like the cracked canyon evoked in tape-hiss cathedral I can still remember the way that I felt weeks in happy in the unexpectedness strange horror difficulty then unfolding inside bereft of structures outside personality to give a track like fluency to burdensome world-weary scram to price cloud stichomythic interplay on how my tongue tended not to dance right moving outside self-consciousness where introductions always take too long and then the main event is ruined in the afterglow of too much praise too many things all happening for the first time at once and the unstable element underneath it all some fascination lost spark need block root contraption obsessed bold break from fractured distraction in this new moment corrupted in judgment lost so long together only finally in exasperation it had to break author-gone-too-far spare expectations in the east and all that weight | and then I came a year later out west to tell you I was gay again like when we first met and it seemed to make sense except of course led nowhere sliding into possibilities seemingly walled off by disagreeable turns in my nature making me repellent or an object of violence to those I most desire so riddled in shame love like a sword and not the beginnings of unfolding slain before life by conditions of censure slicing worlds into what's believable and what just traces slowly the outlines of our future together in some spiral of spiking heat and fueled by distraction seeing structures in themselves as bladed to cut and exclude you at your most secret nature which of course even when unseen is known and felt like an odor of death on the battlefield of conforming to the unspoken secret covenant of despoilment all have resigned to however non-coformingly they carry themselves marching in the name of personal fulfilment little lines of sportive greed made nature in adherence to a self-consumed conception of the other so we sat in the Hare Krishna temple with the ancient talking cat now long dead and I felt a new erratic fragility attempting to leave one phase behind while embarking on another radically different but it was still there in then the whole hollow burning like one of those fad ear candles from the nineties funnels for removing ear accumulate by flame like the inside of that fibrous wax cone I felt an empty cylinder of molten junk deployed only by means of inauthentic media babble bought up in a rush of feelings for cleanliness I was the diode where the allergens all gathered and the best new-fangled sensor and since then nothing hangs desire feels it cuts one way misdrawn to people who have already made their deal not caring for potential what is obviously difficult oh let us be sublime ripped apart Pentheus and all of that come what may I seek long over waters craving cudgeling tender care identical if blasted from the real heart flood of catalogued riposte in dialogic swirl in breaking want's fast equinoctial oblivion where roads open up to no place home paradise you top us utopos clustered in a knotted fist either side it goes back to that night of disinhibition another manic moment of release outside I finally let something of me be available and the consequences could not have been more dire except of course it always could have been worse but even coming towards it so many years later the other person long dead his funeral itself a distant memory I cannot help but feel myself slip and stall into another mood the images of fire and hollowness and darting play all gone replaced with an exasperated memory of my own voice echoing "why did you do that?" and us sitting nearly naked in a bathroom and then me sadly almost weakly "you didn't even do it well" as if that were the issue the aesthetic failure of his act of force the total betrayal of a suddenly radically open friend because he'd struck out earlier with women and I didn't even know this might be possible when first we sat down on the couch like so many other times me lost on the edges of drunkenness and then he was just kissing me so hard it was like nothing I'd ever imagined so much alien in its force its knowing what it wanted in the tongue's objectifying press to say speaking to my throat it was in charge and unmitigatable no parsing of the language possible and later how my friend made jokes to you at a dinner party about me and him how everybody knew except of course what they knew was not the whole thing and even I don't know how we got into the bathroom or when his dick came out into my face but I can still remember gagging with revulsion and being turned suddenly around and him saying "Shut up Stu, you've done this a thousand times before" when in actual point of fact I'd never done anything like this with anyone nothing close I'd never had intercourse with any kind barely kissed a boy in an alley a girl on a trip despite being twenty two years old I was a virgin until that night and all I could say about it was that it happened and there was no thought of recourse or revenge or anything it just sat there like an anger and when I saw him again my friend didn't let me be alone with him despite the pretense shared by us all that everything was fine and we were all friends and later when you and I were together and I imagined my family thrilled I was finally straight when they probably no longer cared I only saw him once on a street corner and he looked tired and broken by disease and drugs and seemed so sad and I knew he was sad and then he wrote me when Derrida died as if to show he still cared about me enough to know that I would care and of course I did but did not know what to make of his writing me then after so long a year after it happened and his life had fallen apart by then expelled from school for mania or something worse and then a few months later he was dead and I was standing at his memorial beside a river and everyone was so sad but unsurprised and you were not well and I felt halted without an effort to break through and just went back to work and we kept on until we couldn't and I was sitting in the abandoned Hare Krishna Temple four years later with you suddenly aflame with hope and love for a new person I already by then should have known this relationship could not amount to much outside my mind and I was the one fully sensate now it seems to me free from self-consciousness and awful in unbalanced want though it was good for then though not for any future and I lean awkward now as all this sits here and I stand looking out the plate glass windows at the people looking in the windows ship rocking with a nervous electricity and all I want to do is get out of this sweltering room and have a smoke there by the stoplights and corner where the traffic passes through that long unmarked section of intersection roadway perfectly like a rock with a rope tied to it flung from one person to another across a gap

In Ogopogo's Arms

Or in his coils, should he have no arms, their, should they have no gender, coils, wrapped tightly as pink inner-ear-skin flares and long blue whiskers brush across the water's surface and you feel it winding you gently, they see you, are yelling already and you are not listening, its body much thicker than any thigh you've felt but suppler somehow, limber like a pitcher's arm but steel, lean within its scaly girth, underneath the muscle ribs as light and hollow as a bird's. The name comes from a popular dance craze of the 1920s, ribs heave as the lithe coil's rapt attention probes, buzzing off in the distant hallway echoes wrung as reverberations hint at the extent of matte, eyes strangely friendly and lively with animated spectral projection, a hint of fleshy fur on the lips that rub along your abdomen like a flexing rubber paint brush, warm-breathed and monstrous almost a scaly dog, lizardine vertebrate, your sighs burst in an ecstatic ekphrasis of joy at unseen object, rondo repetition in the undulating waves of humps bursting the lip of water with fringy ridged backs seemingly downward and on out to the horizon, flat as a ripple after a distance, letting go into the grip of the serpent as it lifts you right out of the lake and into the air for a moment dripping suspended above the logs and branches floating nearby, as much a myth maybe as Marie Antoinette saying "let them eat cake" we agree to sign up to his declaration, camped along the lakeside waiting to crown our newly chosen king, to worship in a writhing wave of bodies Ogopogo's wake as he whips across the surface in circles and ellipses, diving under momentarily and we all hold our breaths and pause until she darts back up, a smile on his lips, her lips, its lips our beloved Empress, mauling trout in glee its silver blue back shimmers in the dusklight as the campfires ignite and we roast marshmallows listening ensorcelled to its long lowing brays beneath dark gray clouds drifting over across the sky, and lying on the beach back on the pebbles, you remember how it was to be held in his tender grip, the way for those few moments there out on the water you felt free in another's control, opened through a kind of submission to the wiles of a previously imaginary snake, a symbol worn like the generalizing factor of the guillotine, a human suffering alone quickly relieved by mechanized death, how nice, delivered as by Moses out of Egypt except directly into Hell, is falling around his resting coils so lovingly, Laocoön embracing his future killer, or tending to the sacred symbol of the stories, the spirit of the waters never figured like this except under the press of capital exchange, we are the sacrifice and Ogopogo moves along into another era to be sought like the meek, we see him taking away our sons on the order of Poseidon but with Athena's full approval, she in all her wisdom knowing how a tame benevolence never long befits a lordly man, a Cecrops born of our lying here together will grant new power to the people through his rule and does so only in the chatter, the insignificance, the tossed out words that populate an ocean to eroticize.

Kleptomaniac Thomas Hardy Wedding

Ypsilanti, Michigan suburb awash in ruined doors | combined apparatuses for drinking out of coal tar | lung switched grey residents out with the flogged door | trick turned on a short corner wallowing besides the small ground | drumming underneath of a discontent that channeled makes the pavement | made the door, an individual never thinks it's his | her labor alienated in amicable patriot's cove America | Descartes' uncertain cribbage | there's a monkey's gland mixed into Yeats. | Fraternal knot dry-heaved out from an earth torn shake blown madrigal piping un-tourniqueted wound | wind streams, larval flaws piping hot pupa flows run off the crass horse gutted fast by wolves left dashed and bashed askance for smaller wings to pluck | we dryads in a glutted wood of luck | full migrants for the tapestries we draw | unbound wind wound earth saw | skit diamond blade shrank straight lane clutch | in trances splashed with runes and such | raiding marks as carve out best the score | and slam the shore | again again with churning beat | set to unseat | freaks bled lexical indexed dead | though likely printed, seen but never read | unwanted résumé | bobs, in an unadulterated way | clenched gutter spittle-lick | crack lineated colors wick | the pages over lets that sharp cut | ululate | but | straight | away rush into inmost day | via spiral staircase, say | "It is here I will tumble down you all" | and spiritedly make your fall | performing shame before technology | lay at the altar of Farfrae | ceding the title as the law demands | accepting alms but no laying on of hands | evaporated unwanted in the cruel | compressing machinery that, as a rule | cares not for you, the individual | plinthing you into a particle | of gear here near the surface. Full | fool. | Staring directly down at yourself in effigy | floating by on a river of glee | flowing freely from a guilting mob | gilting water with painted dummies to fob | off talismanic like a door | an outside that leads inside nothing more | another compartment settled and arranged | a press a grid a form a block unchanged | except by governmental shifts of grip | marked fingerprints that slip | onto a digital slide | you cannot hide | so separate that part of you that's tried | to keep up dignity; dignity died | and went to heaven which, when spied | looks exactly like the past; I lied | the future; timeless darkness either side | of that brief bouncing bit of light wave dancing | while atoms in themselves can keep advancing | with stability | before electrons lose their viability | and gravity too dies | or other planes move in disguise | and skewer us out past | the shallow buzzing of our being here at last.

ز

A Category by Itself

According to legend, his spectacular reign dates to the sixth century CE. There is the fantastical story of his drawing the sword from the stone and of his many adventures with Merlin. In fact, few details about this period in history are known. Britain was being invaded, but by whom and precisely when is a matter of conjecture for historians, and archaeology has thus far been less helpful than we, putting our trust in science, might have hoped it would be. The last we hear, he is taken to Avalon, and then, nothing more.

Along with Richard Carpenter and Donald Trump, he was born in 1946, a year of returning soldiers. That the man's arm is locked around her neck in the famous "spontaneous" street kissing photograph is all you need to know about the relationship between moral victory and entitlement. What moral triumph has not lead immediately to horror, after all? Was his father such a man? Undoubtedly, though the circumstances of his encounter with his mother, still a teenager herself at the time, are destined to remain a complete mystery, his mother having passed away in 2012. If she herself could even say for certain who his father was we cannot ascertain, although the possibility that she was a victim of a drunken, pornography-obsessed father with a well-known sadistic streak has, more than once, been floated by biographers.

Many question if there ever was an Avalon, but in 1191 the monks of Glastonbury Abbey made a fortuitous discovery: King Arthur's "grave." The most celebrated act of archaeology before the time of Heinrich Schliemann, modern historians find the story impossible to authenticate, in part because Henry VIII had Glastonbury Abbey completely razed. As such, skepticism about their claims remains exceedingly high, although over the last century a number of archaeologists have set out to definitively verify or refute the monks' centuries-old claim.

At least in the initial phase of his highly active period, in Seattle, he was impressively organized, having scouted out disposal sites well in advance of the commission of his crimes, picking locations where in several cases, the bodies would not be discovered for more than a year. For whatever reason, when he moved on to Utah and then Colorado, this aspect of the behavior, the meticulous pre-selection of disposal sites, generally picked with both accessibility and potential for discovery very much in mind, seems to gradually fade out, a number of different authors and investigators offering various hypotheses for why this happened. The simplest explanation is, perhaps, geography. Utah lacked the tall coniferous forests familiar to him from Seattle; this was a new territory, and as we shall see, circumstances could only alter in a minor manner his pursuit of his passion.

It would be wrong to understand the 1970s as a "reactionary" decade, one of retrenchment and counter-revolution; that would come with the 1980s. Instead, the 70s seem a decade of purgatory, stagnation, failure, and disillusionment, a period of attempted continuity gone horribly awry, perhaps best typified by the abundance of orange tones and the sound of Jimmy Carter's voice, but the diffusion of a particular strain of seemingly motiveless violence also marks this decade of false hope.

As best we can tell from the available sources, the Merlin mythology has older roots than even the Arthurian legends which have, at their source, an essentially classical core. The similarities, for instance, between the tales of Alexander the Great transmitted throughout many languages across the Middle Ages in the form of The Alexander Romance and Arthur are striking. Most notable, perhaps, is the way in which Arthur's drawing of the sword from out of the stone parallels Alexander's cutting of the fabled Gordian Knot. Alexander's action, however, conveys his cunning, his ruthlessness, his desire to win at any cost, whereas Arthur's action reveals a previously hidden nobility, confers a contested kingship onto the actually proper heir by seemingly supernatural means. The differences between these similar stories are perhaps the best illustration of the differences between the Classical and the Medieval outlooks as regards prophecy, politics, and faith.

> It is undoubtedly true that serial killers look for literature and imagery which they can find stimulating, but oftentimes that material is very far from what we would call "pornography." The single book that has had the greatest influence on serial killers has been, undoubtedly, the Christian Bible, particularly the Book of Revelation. Clearly, the Bible is not pornography, and yet it has had a much greater impact overall on shaping serial killers, in providing them with "inspiring material," than any form of conventional pornography over the course of history.

Similarly, in choosing its foundational myth, a nation generally has a number of options, and there are always considerations that elude us looking back, we historians attempting to piece the real course of events together from the scattered remains of literature and artefacts. One of the chief requirements of a national hero seems to be a kind of originary vagueness, a layer of uncertainty that leaves him open to the application, over the generations, of layers and layers of suddenly necessary mythology. For this reason, historical individuals about whom we know too much, say Ronald Reagan, function poorly when one attempts to build a nationalistic myth around their personhood. Given the enormous amount of empirical evidence we have regarding his life, it is interesting to note that, though Caesar was immediately deified by his contemporaries, his legendary reputation does not nearly approach that of the more nebulous Alexander or of the perhaps entirely fictional King Arthur. A trans-national, cross-cultural example of this phenomenon can of course be seen, most famously, in the figure of Jesus Christ.

I'm satisfied with my blanket statement that I am innocent. No man is truly innocent. We all transgressed in some way in our lives, and as I say, I've been impolite, and there are things that I regret having done in my life, but nothing like the things I think that you're referring to. Have you ever physically harmed anyone? Ever physically harmed anyone? No. No. Again, not in the context I think you're speaking of.

<smiles>

Sure I get angry, I get very, very angry and indignant, I don't like being locked up for something I didn't do, and I don't like my liberty taken away, and I don't like being treated like an animal, and I don't like people walking around and ogling me like I'm some sort of weirdo, because I'm not. Do you think about getting out of here? Well, legally, sure.

<smiles>

Communication within law enforcement is not good. It's bad enough within the states, and then when you start talking about communicating with another state, it's almost non-existent.

Between the time of his initial arrest and his trial for the [ ] kidnapping he converted to Mormonism. The members of the Church who helped him prepare for his conversion said his interest in achieving salvation seemed genuine.

Around this same time his Salt Lake City rooming house was searched, yielding only circumstantial evidence relating to the case in Colorado and the disappearance of [ ] from the play in Bountiful. However, he would later admit that, had they thought to search the shed out behind the house, they would have found a cache of polaroid photos of his victims posed, in nature and in his apartment, in various degrading ways. As soon as the search was over, he destroyed these photos, and any trace of one of his two Idaho victims who is to this day unidentified.

His two
escapes
from
Colorado
were not
motivated
so much
by a
desire to
be free as
they were
motivated
by a
desire to
be free to
kill.

In the *Historia Brittonum* it is said that at the Battle of Badon Hill, Arthur personally killed 960 men.

Lord knows what the little creatures up there did, what the animals would have done, but I think, well let me start with one, let me start with the unidentified remains, this is where I'm, the presence of the officers down here is unnerving...

<whispers>

I just said that the [   ] girl's head was severed and taken up the road twenty five to fifty yards and buried in a location about ten yards west of the road on a rocky hillside.

...I was moving up the alley using a, uh, a briefcase and some crutches and a young woman walked down. I saw her round the north end of the block into the alley and stopped for a moment and then keep on walking down the alley toward me and about halfway down the block I encountered her and asked her to help me carry the briefcase which she did and we walked back up the alley across the street, turned right on the sidewalk in front of, I think, the fraternity house on the corner there, uh, rounded the corner to the left and went north on 47th...well midway in the block there used to be, you know, one of those parking lots they used to make out of burned down houses in that area...it was to the car <sighs> uh...basically when I reached the car what happened was I knocked her, knocked her unconscious with the crowbar.

Where'd you have that?

By the car.

Outside?

Outside. In back of...the car.

Did she see it?

No. And then uh there was some <whispers> some handcuffs there *along with the crowbar...the crowbar...I handcuffed her and put her in the driver's I mean the passenger's side of the car and drove away.*

Was she alive or dead then?

Oh no, she was quite, she was unconscious, but she was very much alive. One of the things that makes it a little bit, uh, among the things that makes it difficult is that at this point she was quite lucid talking about things about some...

<laughs>

it's funny, it's not funny, but it's odd, the kinds of things people say under those circumstances, and she thought, she said that she thought she had a Spanish test the next day, and she thought that I'd taken her to help tutor me for her Spanish test. Kinda odd. An odd thing to say.

> *The long and short of it I mean I'll I'm gonna try and make this get there by degrees the long and short of it is I again knocked her unconscious and strangled her and drove her into about ten yards into the small grove of trees that was there.*

Talk about details coming back, I couldn't find one of the shoes. So I thought it was there, but it wasn't. So I went back. This was the, this was the next day. Got on my bicycle, rode back to that little parking lot. I knew there were police all over the place by that time, but I was kind of... nervous, and I'll tell you why in a minute, because I'd left, and my car had been parked there so they may have seen it and now if something was found there it might connect me. So I went back to that parking lot and I found both pierced, the pierced earrings and the shoe laying in the parking lot at about 5 in the afternoon, so I surreptitiously gathered them up and rode off.

I won't beat around the bush with you any more because I'm just tired and I just want to get back and go to sleep so let me just tell you, I'm, I know that, this part of the forest, buried up in there but, nothing identifiable, probably just, literally, bones, but, the head, however, the, the skull, it wouldn't be there.

Where is it?

It's nowhere.

It's nowhere?

Well, I don't know, I'm not trying to be flippant, it's just, it's nowhere. It's, it's, it's, it's in a category by itself, in, in that ah, it was… Now I just assumed this was, something you just can't I don't know, I can see the headlines now but, ah, ah…

[   ], there's not going to be any details. What you told me about [   ] isn't going to be known. I got parents out there that don't even want to know the details.

Well I know, I know…

He wants to know, and I want to know for my own good.

Well, it was incinerated, and it was, just ah, an exception ah, a strange exception, but, ah, it was incinerated.

Where'd you incinerate it?

Well it, ah, I don't know the address of the place, I never want to tell this incident, but I promised myself I'd never tell this because it would ah, I, I thought, that, of, of all the things I did to this woman this was probably the one she would least likely to forgive me for, poor [   ]….

Uh, huh…

In her fireplace, ah, it's not that humorous, but um, in the fireplace in that house…

Burned it all up?

Down to the last ash, in a fit of, you know, paranoia and cleanliness, what have you, just vacuumed down all the ashes. That's the twist.

Arthur's death, at the hands of his nephew Mordred who is also killed in their encounter, has a distinctly Theban element, recalling, as it does, the similarly simultaneous deaths of Polynices and Eteocles. Like the Greek brothers, at issue was a royal partnership, Mordred having betrayed Arthur while the latter was abroad in France dealing with the aftermath of Lancelot's seduction of Guinevere. In later versions of the story, it is alleged that, as in the Greek story, Mordred and Arthur were related through incest, although in this case it was incest between siblings and not between a mother and a son. Unlike in Thebes but again very much like the tale of Alexander the Great, Arthur's death leads to the scattering and destruction of his kingdom; what the myth of his return, so heavily emphasized by Victoria and her husband Albert, implies is that the reunification of this mythical, Arthurian Britain is in fact a matter of divine necessity. His promised return again suggests the influence of the Gospels on this later story, which is perhaps, in the final estimation best understood as a synthesis of Classical Myth with Christian Parable after all, as has been suggested by everyone from Curtius to Auerbach to Lukács to Bakhtin, though we should, of course, be careful about drawing general conclusions from particular examples.

Less known in America, but also prolifically active in this era, Pedro Alonso López confessed to murdering over 300 girls who were between the ages of 8 and 12. His confessions, made while he was imprisoned to a jailhouse priest, an informant, and a single traveling Canadian journalist, explain that he committed these crimes traveling between Colombia, Ecuador, and Peru over the course of the previous seven years, which would put the beginning of his killing spree sometime in 1973.

When one dies, one totally loses his emotions, his vision, his ability to see, a death that you can forget who you are, everything you did is now darkness.

He was paraded in front of the cameras where he would philosophize, abstractly, on matters of life in this manner.

López: *This will be history, right?*

Reporter: *Yes.*

He offered to lead police to all of the graves, across eleven Ecuadorian provinces, a journey that would reveal the truth behind this seemingly insignificant man.

During the course of the investigations, López was disguised as a police officer. They found a completed skeleton, heavily decomposed, the bones damaged by ten months of wind and rain, exposed, besides a viaduct. This was only the beginning of an unprecedented sequence of horrors. The police would bribe him for information using cigarettes, chicken, and beer, though this was probably unnecessary because, in the nature of things, the killer seemed to take a peculiar delight in leading them to every single grave. At no point did he express any remorse, at one grave even attempting to pose for a photo with one of the victim's skulls tucked under has arm. In all the police would discover 57 bodies in Ecuador.

López had never met his own father, the father having been shot and killed in 1948 during one of the many swings of political fortune during that period in Colombia, known to historians today as "La Violencia." He was a well-regarded student, although he would later claim to have been brutally abused by his mother. His mother, he insisted, had been a prostitute for a time, and he would recount witnessing her being abused by her clients. Soon after, he ran away from home, henceforward making his home on the streets of Bogotá.

> *My life has been dishonest because of being abandoned.*

Soon he had joined a child gang, a violent and inadequate surrogate family, fighting with knives and belts over territory, keeping company with diseased mongrel dogs and rats, all of them delinquents, hardening to a brutal and jagged edge their personhoods. One night, having been offered a place to sleep for the night by an older man, López was taken to an abandoned building and repeatedly raped.

> *I have always wanted to punish those responsible.*

At the age of 10 he was approached by an American couple who offered him a home, enrolling him in a school for orphans, where for a time he lived a stable existence, until he was sexually assaulted by a male teacher which caused him to flee back into the streets.

Later on, in prison for stealing a car, he murdered several fellow prisoners with a knife after they raped him. Judging his actions to be self-defense, the authorities added no time to his sentence.

He would employ charm, asking for directions; he never used force to kidnap his victims, just persuasion. Unlike his American contemporary, López would spend the night with his victims alive, waiting until the morning to strangle them. This behavior becomes all the more impossible to imagine when one recalls the extremely young age of his murder victims.

By 1979, the police finally began to admit that the large number of missing girls could not all be runaways. The disappearances at last were mentioned on television, in the media.

> Victim's Father: *For me it was very tragic.*

As a result of publicity, López was captured by an angry mob in a market, in a situation strangely similar to the capture, in a bus station, of Richard Ramirez in Los Angeles some five years later. Due to the peculiarities of Ecuadorian law, his confession to the murder of some 57 girls, combined with his guilty plea, meant that he would be sentenced in the same way as if he had only confessed to murdering 1 person, and to a maximum of 16 years.

In his prison interviews, López put all of the blame for his crimes on the society that failed to nurture him. Others speculate on a dark, quasi-Nietzschean motivation behind López's killings: he was "weeding out ugly or weak members of a society" he perceived as being in need of strengthening. This notion is, of course, completely ridiculous. He always spoke about his victims as if he loved them, as if, in murdering them, he had saved them from a life of poverty. At different times he would claim the crimes had been committed by an alternate personality. Prison psychiatric examinations determined López to be a psychopath, someone with a severely deficient capacity for empathy.

> *You ask me if I felt anything while asphyxiating certain persons? Well, no. It's strange, no? Someone who shoots another with a gun, and the other person feels the pain of the bullet, is the shooter going to feel the same pain?*

The law did not allow for consecutive sentences. After 14 years, he was released. He was only 45 years old.

> *I have always lived in poverty, and I have ambitions of being powerful one day, or of great importance. I understand what I have done. There is no going back.*

Victim's Mother: *I wanted revenge. I wanted to break him into pieces because he killed my baby.*

López was deported to Colombia. He was detained in a psychiatric hospital until 1998, at which point he was released. He briefly visited his mother, selling her chair and bed, and disappeared. He has not been seen since.

> He is suspected in at least one additional murder, committed in 2002, in Espinal, Colombia, the city of his birth.

Genetic averages across the generations bear this
out
with complacency it is natural
nature out beyond that bit of shrubbery
contains nothing
circles spasmodically nothing
by action driving seafoam
into the air
emergent clouds of transfixed materials suspended
between states
communicating elements arranged
groups conversant across time
nothing besides these scattered remains adequate
tools for our cables
long long leveled
wired beneath the ridges of the Atlantic
tunnels like marionette strings lifting arms
pressed into a calm blade
a murderous whiteness at wave crest
crashing hard against the stable connections
beneath the underwater earth
new and immense volcanic mountains rise
the attitudes of pressure
riveting stretched of this globe about to burst

Acknowledgements

Poems from this collection first appeared, in some cases in slightly different forms, in the following journals:

"The Will to Know" in *SAND*
"The Amerika Rocket" and "Big Pressures Were There" in *FLAG + VOID*
"Rodan" in *Fjords Review*
"Chandeliers" in *Powder Keg*
"Misspelled Name Love Note" in *White Wall Review*
"Clarence Thomas Coke Can" in *inter|rupture*
"Kleptomaniac Thomas Hardy Wedding" in *Posit*

Pieces in this book draw on language from documentary sources, reworking the language to suit the ends of the poems. Sources for these poems are all available on youtube, and they include:

Jack the Ripper – The Definitive Story
Interview with Julian Pearce, November 13, 2015, CNN
Murder Hotel: The Story of America's First Serial Killer
The Last Days of Julius Caesar
In Search of Athelstan, BBC Documentary by Michael Wood
Germany after the War: 1945-49
Robert D. Keppel interview with Theodore Robert Bundy
Pedro Alonso López: The Monster of the Andes

Special thanks to my parents, my siblings, Rob, Chris, Chris, John, Andrew, Evan, Catherine, Armando, George, Lucy, Maureen, Jake, Harold, Charlie, Hai, Marco, Jesse, Jamie, Michael, Jen, David, Josh, and to all the editors and readers who have supported my work..

Linocut print illustrations by the author.

MASTODON TITLES

FICTION

A Diet of Worms by Erik Rasmussen
The Pleasures of Queueing by Erik Martiny
Life During Wartime by Katie Rogin
Pages From The Textbook Of Alternate History by Phong Nguyen

MEMOIR

Gatsby's Child by Dorin Schumacher

POETRY

Communicatingroups by Stu Watson
Give a Girl Chaos by Heidi Seaborn

SPECIALTY

Casanova by Sonia Hensler
Manson Family Paper Doll Book by John Reed

www.ingramcontent.com/pod-product-compliance
Lightning Source LLC
Chambersburg PA
CBHW022118090426
42743CB00008B/900